# Mathematics 3

# *Mathematics 3*

Apple Pie's Tuition Programme

PARTRIDGE

**To order additional copies of this book, contact**
Toll Free 800 101 2657 (Singapore)
Toll Free 1 800 81 7340 (Malaysia)
orders.singapore@partridgepublishing.com

www.partridgepublishing.com/singapore

# TEST 1

## Section A

1. 90 hundreds is the same as _____

   a) 9 000          b) 9500
   c) 1 900          d) 900

2. _____ - 739 = 4 560

   a) 4 359          b) 5 299
   c) 5 389          d) 3 821

3. 5 thousands 30 ones is 225 fewer than _____ .

   a) 4 895          b) 5 255
   c) 4 430          d) 5 700

4. 1500ml of juice can fill up _____ 250ml-cups.

   a) 5              b) 6
   c) 7              d) 8

5.  $8 \times 9 = $ _____

    a) 48                 b) 54
    c) 72                 d) 56

6.  Jones has 155 sweets. She gives the sweets equally to 10 children. How many sweets will there be left over?

    a) 9                  b) 0
    c) 5                  d) 2

7.  _____ $- 1/6 = 1/2$

    a) 2/6                b) 1
    c) 2/3                d) 1/4

8.  3 cans of drink cost $4. 12 such cans of drink would cost $_____ .

    a) 24                 b) 16
    c) 28                 d) 12

9.  John finishes his homework in 1h 20min. His sister finishes 30 minutes earlier. John's sister has finished her work in _____ minutes.

    a) 50                 b) 90
    c) 100                d) 170

10. The perimeter of a square is 30cm. Each side of the square is _____ cm.

    a) 5                     b) 7 1/2

    c) 7                     d) 5 1/2

# Section B

1. _____ ones _____ tens _____ hundreds _____ thousands = 4 589

2. 1 310 less than 3 664 is _____

3. 10 000m - 8 175m = _____ km _____ m

4. 4m 8cm = _____ cm

5. 1, 4, 9, _____, _____, 36, _____, _____

6. Arrange in order. Begin with the greatest.

   2400g, 1/2kg, 3400g, 2kg 150g, 810g

7.    Draw 15 mins to 9am.

8.    Color 1/8 of the rectangle.

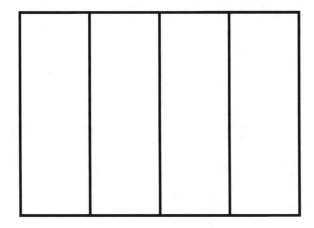

9.    Simplify 12/16.

10.   John has an equal number of $5- and $2-notes. He has 60 of them altogether. John has $_____ in all.

11.   634 / 8 =

12.   Peter spent ½ of his money and Mary ¾ of her money. They found they had spent same amount of money. Who had more money at first? _____

13.   9 kg 450g = 2 kg 800g + ___ kg ___ g

14.   The worker has 8 l 50ml of paint in 5 containers equally. Each of the containers has ___ l _____ ml of paint.

15.   Mother went shopping at 2.45pm and returned home at 5.15pm. For how long had Mother been shopping? _____ h _____ min

# Section C

1.  Samy bought a shirt cost $15.90 and a pair of shoes which cost $50 more than his shirt. Mary bought a book cost $12.50. How much had Samy and Mary spent?

2.  In a box, there are 145 plastic thumb thacks. The steel thumb thacks are 82 fewer than the plastic ones.

    a) How many thumb thacks are there altogether?

    b) End of the day, only 25 thumb thacks are left. How many thumb thacks have been used?

3.  Sam has some ceiling fans which have 3 or 4-blades. The 3-blade fans are twice as many as the 4-blade ones. Sam counted 30 blades for all his fans. How many fans has he?

4. The white rice weighed 50kg. It was packed into 4 equal bags.

   a. Find the weight of each bag of rice.

   b. How much rice was left after the packing?

5. Ali has a retail shop. He usually gets his goods from the warehouse in his van. Sometimes he cycles, takes a bus or takes a cab to the warehouse for his goods.

Study the graph and answer the questions :

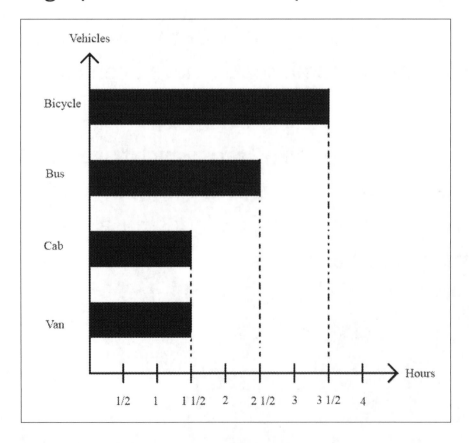

a. How long does Ali usually need to travel to the warehouse in his van?

_____

b. How much faster if he drives than he cycles?

_____

c. On a certain day, Ali took a bus at 5.30am. On the way the bus broke down for 18 mins before it continued its journey. At what time did he reach the warehouse?

_____

d. In the graph, the cab or Ali's van will travel 30km to reach the warehouse. If Ali drove faster in his van to reach the warehouse ½ h earlier, how many km must he be ahead of the cab?

# Answers Test 1

## Section A

1.  a      2.  b      3.  b      4.  b      5.  c
6.  c      7.  c      8.  b      9.  a      10.  b

## Section B

1.  9, 8, 5, 4      2.  2354            3.  1 km 825 m
4.  408 cm      5.  16, 25, 49, 64
6.  3400 g, 2400 g, 2kg 150 g, 810 g, 1/2 kg
7.  8.45am      8.
9.  12/16 = 6/8 = 3/4
10.  $210            11.  79 rem 2    12.  Peter  13.  6kg 650g
14.  1 l 610 ml    15.  2 h 30min

## Section C

1.      $15.90 + $50 = $65.90
        $65.90 + $12.50 + $15.90 = $94.30

They had spent $94.30.

2.    a) 145 - 82 = 63
         145 + 63 = 208
There are 208.


      b) 208 - 25 = 183
183 thumb thacks have been used.


3.    6 x 3 = 18
      3 × 4 = 12
      18 + 12 = 30
      6 + 3 = 9
He has 9 fans.


4.    50kg / 4 = 12 rem 2
      a. The weight of each bag of rice was 12kg.
      b. The weight of the rice left was 2kg.


5.    a. 1½ h

5b.   3 1/2 - 1 1/2 = 2 h faster
5c.   5 h 30 min + 18 min = 5 h 48 min
      5.48 + 2h 30min = 8.18am
5d.   30 / 3 = 10
      30 / 2 = 15
      15 - 10 = 5 km ahead

# TEST 2

## Section A

1. The value of digit '4' in 4965 is ____.

   a) 40 hundreds          b) 40 tens
   c) 40 thousands         d) 400 ones

2. Ben paid $146.85 for his racket. Jim paid $56 more than Ben. How much is Jim's racket?

   a) $202.85          b) $438.85
   c) $349.80          d) $364.30

3. 3m 40cm + 8m 80cm =

   a) 11m 20cm          b) 12m 80cm
   c) 12m 40cm          d) 12m 20cm

4. 8 mins to three in noon is the same as

   a) 2.30pm          b) 2.52pm
   b) 3.08pm          d) 1.48pm

5.  There are 3 400 students. 1 300 of them are wearing ties. How many more students are there not wearing ties?

    a) 700            b) 2 100
    c) 800            d) 1 000

6.  Sally baked 90 cupcakes. To put into boxes of 6, she needed ____ boxes.

    a) 15             b) 25
    c) 35             d) 20

7.  1 188 / _____ = 396

    a) 7              b) 8
    c) 3              d) 4

8.  98 tens more than 2336 is _____ .

    a) 2 443          b) 3 316
    c) 1 436          d) 3 036

9.  1/3 is the same as ____

    a) 3/9            b) 3/6
    c) 3/5            d) 2/5

10. 7 groups of eights is equal to ____ .

    a) 4 groups of fourteens.
    b) 3 groups of twelves
    c) 2 groups eighteens
    d) 9 groups of nines

# Section B

1.      856 + _____ = 4 326

2.      Write in words.

   6078

   992

3.      4 thousands 40 ones = _____ x 2

4.      Digit '3' in 3 719 is in the _____ place.

5.      8 tomatoes each weighed equally totalled 840g. 72 such tomatoes weighed _____ g.

6.      8kg 150g = 10kg - _____ kg _____ g

7.      4 560m = _____ km _____ m

8.      Reorder. Begin with the smallest.

   4106, 1867, 9046, 82 tens 60 ones, 2 thousands

9. Complete the number pattern.

   7, 21, 35, _____, 63, _____, _____

10. Which fraction shows every length of a square?

    2/5, 4/4, 1/4, 3/8

11. 1/2 - 1/6 = _____ / 3

12. Peter went to the library at 10.15am. He stayed at the library for 5 h 15 min. At what time did he leave the library? _____

13. There is 9 litres of syrup. It is poured equally into 2 containers. There is _____ l _____ ml in each container.

14. The fishmonger sold every 100g of fish at 90 cents. Mother bought 550g of them. She had paid $_____.

15. The chest of drawers is 76cm in height. The cupboard is 1m 65cm in height. It is _____ cm higher.

# Section C

1. In a pet shop, 3 times as many puppies as kittens were sold. If the shop sold away 4000 of both pets, how many kittens in the shop were sold?

2. There are 140 plants in 7 rows equally.

   a) How many plants are there in each row?
   b) The gardener rearranges the plants in 5 rows equally, how many more plants are there in each row now?

3. There are 28 marbles in a bottle. How many marbles are there in 150 such bottles?

4. A cyclist will usually take 1 h 10 mins to reach the station. A bus will reach 30 mins earlier for the same journey. If the bus and the cyclist start the journey at 8.30 am, what time will the bus reach the station?

5. There are 16 birds. 3 of them are green. There are 5 more black ones than the yellow ones. How many yellow birds are there?

# Answers Test 2

| Section A | Section B |
|---|---|
| 1. a | 1. 3470 |
| 2. a | 2. Six thousand and seventy-eight |
| 3. d | Nine hundred and ninety-two |
| 4. b | 3. 2020 |
| 5. c | 4. Thousands |
| 6. a | 5. 7560g |
| 7. c | 6. 1kg 850g |
| 8. b | 7. 4 km 560 m |
| 9. a | 8. 82 tens 60 ones, 1867, 2 thousands, 4106, 9046 |
| 10. a | 9. 49, 77, 91 |
| | 10. 1/4 |
| | 11. 2/6 = 1/3 |
| | 12. 3.30pm |
| | 13. 4l 500ml |
| | 14. $4.95 |
| | 15. 89cm |

## Section C

1.  4000 / 4 = 1000
    1000 kittens were sold.

2.  140 / 7 = 20
    a. There are 20 plants in each row.
    140 / 5 = 28
    28 - 20 = 8
    b. There are 8 more plants in each row now.

3.  28 x 100 = 2800
    28 x 50 = 1400
    2800 + 1400 = 4200
    There are 4200 marbles in all.

4.  1h 10mins = 70 mins
    70 mins - 30 mins = 40mins
    40 mins past 8.30 am is 9.10 am
    The bus will reach at 9.10 am.

5.  16 - 3 = 13
    13 - 5 = 8
    8 / 2 = 4
    There are 4 yellow birds.

# TEST 3

## Section A

1.  20 tens + 57 hundreds =

    a) 3400  b) 7750
    c) 2057  d) 5900

2.  96 divided by _____ is 12

    a) 6  b) 7
    c) 8  d) 9

3.  6892 is 920 fewer than _____ .

    a) 5972  b) 7812
    b) 4632  d) 8082

4.  Dick has 45 apple pies. He wants to put them in 6 boxes equally. How many apples pies will he have left over?

    a) 9  b) 4
    c) 3  d) 5

5. Jean, Sally and Betty each pay $19.50 for the dinner. How much is the bill for them?

   a) fifty-eight dollars and fifty cents
   b) twenty-eight dollars and ninety cents
   c) eighty-five dollars
   d) nineteen dollars and fifty cents

6. $1 - 2/9 =$

   a) 3/9             b) 4/9
   c) 5/9             d) 7/9

7. A rectangle measured 18cm × 13cm. What was its perimeter?

   a) 96 cm           b) 62 cm
   c) 31 cm           d) 43 cm

8. 7 1/4 hrs = _____ mins

   a) 350             b) 490
   c) 435             d) 515

9.  Ben ran 8 km. He was 25m behind Judy. Judy had run _____ .

    a) 8000 m        b) 8250 m
    c) 8500 m        d) 8025 m

10. June has to travel 12 stations from her house to the library. She has travelled 1/3 of the stations. How many stations has June travelled?

    a) 5                        b) 4
    c) 3                        d) 9

# Section B

1.  Write in words.

    8932 -

    1344 -

2.  Karen collected 285 more stickers than John. John had collected 165 stickers. They had collected _____ stickers altogether.

3.  Sandra has bought 4 similar packets of prawn crackers weighed 700g. Sandra has _____ g of crackers in each of her packets.

4.  Each container has 48 teabags. How many tea bags are there in five such containers? _____ tea bags.

5.  If you save $15 every week, you will take _____ days to save $60 ?

6.  7 thousands 9 tens 15 ones is _____

7.    Draw a line BD measured 16cm long.

8.    _____ / 333 = 4 rem 1

9.    3/5 is equivalent to _____/20

10.   3600, 600, _____, 30, 10, _____

11.   5kg 180g - ____kg ____g = 680g

12.   Arrange in order. Begin with the smallest.

      3m, 2m 9cm, 280cm, 2 1/2m, 600cm

13.   1/8 + _____ = 5/8 (your answer in simplest form)

14.   A rectangular pool has a length of 8m. Its breath is 2m shorter. The area of the pool is ____m sq.

15.   The digit '2' in 2 569 has a value of ____.

# Section C

1. George works 4 hours every day. Each hour he earns $8. How many days has he worked when he earns $320?

2. The chairs are 3 times as many as the desks in the hall. There are 45 chairs in all. How many more desks are needed so that there is an equal number of chairs and desks?

3. The cabbages and spinach weighed 1850g. The cabbages weighed 600g heavier. What was the weight of the spinach?

4. Mary bought 4 muffins. They cost $6.

   a. How much was each muffin?
   b. How much were 25 such muffins?

5. Mother has baked a pizza. She cuts 1/6 of the pizza for each of her 3 children. What is the fraction of her pizza left?

# Answers Test 3

## Section A

1. d        2. c        3. b        4. c        5. a
6. d        7. b        8. c        9. d        10. b

## Section B

1.  Eight thousand, nine hundred and thirty-two
One thousand, three hundred and forty-four

2.  615        3.  175g        4.  240        5.  28 days   6.  7105
7.    8.  1333   9.  12/20      10.  120, 5   11.  4 kg 500 g

12.  2m 9cm, 2 1/2m, 280cm, 3m, 600cm
13.  1/2   14.  48 m sq   15.  2000

## Section C

1.  320 / 8 = 40

40 / 4 = 10
He has worked for 10 days.

2.  45 / 3 = 15

15 x 2 = 30
30 more desks are needed.

3.  1850 - 600 = 1250

1250 / 2 = 625
The spinach weighed 625g.

4.  $6 / 4 = $1.50

a. Each muffin was $1.50.

24 / 4 = 6
6 × $6 = $36
$36 + $1.50 = $37.50

b. 25 muffins cost $37.50.

5.  1/6 + 1/6 + 1/6 = 3/6

1 - 3/6 = 3/6 = 1/2
The fraction of pizza left is 1/2.

# TEST 4

## Section A

1.  Johnny saves $0.50 daily. He will have saved $\_\_\_\_\_
    in 40 days.

    a) 25           b) 20
    c) 50           d) 30

2.  7 920 is the same as

    a) 7 thousands 92 tens
    b) 70 hundreds 9 tens
    c) 7 thousands 9 hundreds 2 ones
    d) 7 thousands 92 ones

3.  A square has a length of 14 cm. What is the perimeter
    of the square?

    a) 14 × 14        b) 14 × 2
    c) 14 + 4         d) 14 × 4

4.  Mr Yang installed two similar water heaters. They had cost him $725. Mr Yang was paying $_____ for each of them.

    a) 362.50          b) 400.10
    c) 350.50          d) 225.20

5.  A rectangle measured 24 × 20cm. Its area is greater than _____ cm sq.

    a) 700             b) 500
    c) 600             d) 400

6.  Diane has $60. She wants to buy a blouse costs $89.90. How much more does she need?

    a) $29.90          b) $20.90
    c) $24.80          d) $15.90

7.  385cm + 16cm =

    a) 4m 10m          b) 3m 9cm
    c) 5m 8cm          d) 4m 1cm

8. 1/4 of the pizza weighed 67g. What was the weight of the whole pizza?

   a) 268g            b) 400g
   c) 184g            d) 320g

9. The simplest form of 16/20 is

   a) 5/6             b) 4/5
   c) 8/10            d) 5/4

10. The time now is 3.05pm. Mary's watch is 20 mins slow. What is the time on Mary's watch?

    a) 3.00pm         b) 2.40pm
    c) 3.25pm         d) 2.45pm

# Section B

Write in number.

1.    Four thousand Eight hundred and fifty-nine _____

62 hundreds 50 tens 8 ones _____

2.    349 - 286 + 115 =

3.    5 tomatoes can make 80ml of juices. 15 such tomatoes can make _____ ml of juices.

4.    9 km 150m = _____ m

5.    7 l 20 ml - 2 l 100ml = _____ l _____ ml

6.    The bakery sold 23 tens egg tarts and 9 tens fewer cream tarts than the egg tarts. The bakery had sold away _____ tarts altogether.

7.  Mdm Tan is 57 years old. She is 3 times as old as Betty. How old is Betty?

    _____ years old

8.  _____ divided by 6 = 76

9.  Measure the line AB and draw a perpendicular line to it.

    A                                              B

    _____

10. Reorder. Begin with the greatest.

    9095, 3925, 9352, 2935, 3592

11. Jean reached her grandparents' house at 9.15am. When the time was 11.50am, Jean went home. Jean stayed _____ h _____ mins at her grandparents' house.

12. _____ tens - 431 = 5 hundreds 49 ones

13. Samy jogged round the field 3 times. Each round measured 500m. Samy had jogged _____ km _____ m in the field.

14. Complete the number pattern.

    9 + 9, 10 + 8, _____, 12 + 6, _____

15. 5/12 - 1/3 = _____

# Section C

1.  A shop sold 350 toys in 3 months. It sold 80 more toys in January than February. In March it sold 50 toys.

    a) How many toys had the shop sold in the first two months?

    b) How many toys had the shop sold in January?

2.  Kevin is buying 550g of chocolates for his party. The chocolates is being selling at $4 for every 50g.

    How much does Kevin's chocolates cost?

3.  Because of his mistakes, James has to replace 3 bottles of drinks in each of the cartons. He has finished replacing 24 bottles of drinks and left 90 bottles to go.

    How many cartons of drinks are there for James?

4.  Jane had 3 cups of cooking cream each measured 250ml. Jane used some of the cream and left 400ml of it. How much cooking cream had Jane used?

5. After mother gave Bob $30, he found he had $80 more than his sister and his sister also found she had half as much as James. How much money had James at first?

# Answers Test 4

## Section A

1. b     2. a     3. d     4. a     5. d
6. a     7. d     8. a     9. b     10. d

## Section B

1. 4859, 6708
2. 178
3. 240 ml
4. 9150 m
5. 4 l 920 ml
6. 370
7. 19
8. 456
9. 11 cm
10. 9352, 9095, 3925, 3592, 2935
11. 2h 35min
12. 98
13. 1km 500m
14. 11+7, 13+5
15. 1/12

## Section C

1.  350 - 50 = 300

a. The shop sold 300 toys.
300 - 80 = 220
220 / 2 = 110
110 + 80 = 190

b. The shop sold 190 toys in January.

2.  4 x 11 = $44
Kevin's chocolates cost $44.

3.  24 + 90 = 114
114 / 3 = 38
There are 38 cartons

4.  250ml x 3 = 750
750ml - 400ml = 350 ml
She used 350 ml.

5.  $80 - $30 = $50
$50 + $80 = $130.
James had $130 at first.

# TEST 5

## Section A

1.  30 bottles of perfume each contain 35ml. The total volume of the perfume is

    a) 900ml      b) 1 050ml
    c) 3 150ml      d) 2 100ml

2.  95 tens = _____ - 875

    a) 970      b) 1825
    c) 1685      d) 1950

3.  2 089 divided by 6 has a remainder of

    a) 2      b) 7
    c) 9      d) 1

4.  5 x _____ = 780 / 3

    a) 52      b) 60
    c) 25      d) 48

5.   A blue blouse on offer costs $18.50. It is $9.50 cheaper. What is the original cost?

   a) $21.00          b) $28.00
   c) $30.50          d) $27.40

6.   3/4 is greater than

   a) 1/2             b) 1
   c) 7/8             d) 5/6

7.   1605 more than _____ is 3890.

   a) 20 hundreds 28 tens 5 ones
   b) 22 hundreds 2 tens 5 ones
   c) 28 hundreds 5 ones
   d) 20 hundreds 18 tens 5 ones

8.   A wall tile is 4 cm sq. A worker can lay _____ such wall tiles for an area of 296 cm sq.

   a) 82              b) 65
   c) 48              d) 74

9. The worker has worked for 525 mins. He has worked as long as

   a) 5 h 45 min
   b) 7 h 25 min
   c) 8 h 45 min
   d) 9 h 15 min

10. A ribbon measured 3m 20cm long. It is cut for 7 parcels. Every parcel will need 50cm. The ribbon is _____ cm shorter for the last parcel.

    a) 20          b) 30
    b) 40          d) 10

# Section B

1. The value of digit '3' in 3 685 is _____ hundreds.

2. Write in words.

   7058

   3416

3. 8595 = _____ thousands _____ hundreds _____ tens 15 ones

4. There are 4800g of cabbages. The cauliflowers weigh 208g heavier than the cabbages. What is the weight of the cauliflowers? _____ kg _____ g

5. 
   ```
        8 ___ 6
     ×       9
     --------------
        7 ___ 3 4
     --------------
   ```

6. Carrie collected 2256 stamps. She has three times as many stamps as Linda. How many more stamps has Carrie? _____ more stamps.

7. _____ $/ 8 = 53$ rem 3

8. Circle the biggest odd number.

    9346, 3567, 2989, 1943, 4290

9. 5950 kg = 9 kg - ____ kg ____ g

10. 10 km = 8000 m + _____ m

11. In an hour, Susan sews 4 flowers and Mary sews 6. How much faster is Mary for each of her sewings? _____ mins

12. Arrange in order. Begin with the smallest.

    4m 90cm, 8m, 6m 53cm, 530cm, 70cm

13. Mary bought two 875-ml bottles of milk. She drank 125ml each day. How many days could the bottles of milk last?

_____ days

14. Write 3 equivalent fractions for 3/5.

15. Complete the number pattern.

10, 9, 8 1/2, _____, 7, 6, _____

# Section C

1. There are 14 motorcycles and cars. If there are 8 motorcycles, how many wheels are there altogether?

2. Jar A has 400ml more fruit juice than Jar B. Jar A has 3000ml of juice. How much juice is there in both jars? (Give your answer in l and ml)

3. Jasmine bought a drawing board cost $34.90. She bought some pens which cost $17 more than the board. Then she left $13.20. How much money had Jasmine at first?

4. Mother left 2/7 of her flour after making a cake.

   a) What was the fraction of flour mother had used?
   b) How much more in fraction had mother used her flour than left?

5. Mr Lim sells noodles at his stall in market. Each packet of his noodles can serve 4 customers.

Study the graph and answer the questions:

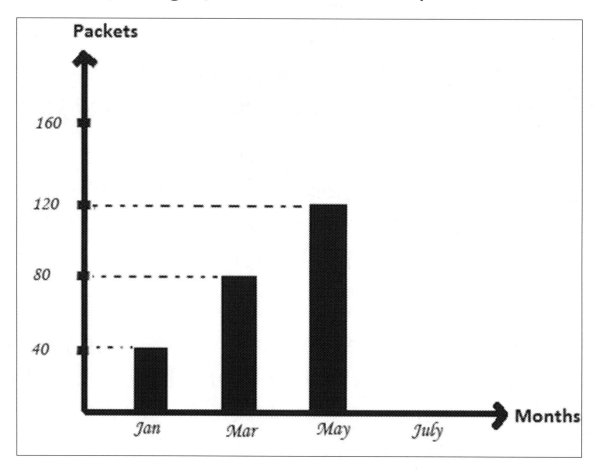

a) How many packets of noodles had he cooked in March?

b) How many packets of noodles had he used in January and May?

c) How many customers had he served in May?

d) Mr Lim served 600 customers in July. Draw in the graph the packets of noodles he served for the customers.

e) Mr Lim ordered 100 packets of noodles every month. How many packets of noodles has he left after July?

# Answers Test 5

## Section A

1. b      2. b      3. d      4. a      5. b
6. a      7. a      8. d      9. c      10. b

## Section B

1. 30
2. Seven thousand and fifty-eight
Three thousand, four hundred and sixteen
3. 8, 5, 8
4. 5 kg 8 g
5. 2, 4
6. 1504
7. 427
8. 3567
9. 3 kg 50 g
10. 2000
11. 5 mins
12. 70cm, 4m 90cm, 530cm, 6m 53cm, 8m
13. 14

14. 6/10, 9/15, 12/20
15. 7 1/2, 5 1/2

Section C

1.      14 - 8 = 6

        8 × 2 = 16

        6 x 4 = 24

        16 + 24 = 40

There are 40 wheels.

2.      3000ml - 400ml = 2600ml

        2600ml + 3000ml = 5600ml

There is 5 l 600 ml of juice.

3.      $34.90 + $17 = $51.90

        $34.90 + $13.20 + $51.90 = $100.00

Jasmine had $100 at first.

4.      1 - 2/7 = 5/7

        a. Mother had used 5/7 of flour.

        5/7 - 2/7 = 3/7

        b. Mother used 3/7 more flour.

5.  a) 80 packets
    b) 40. + 120 = 160 packets
    c) 120 x 4 = 480 customers
    d) 600 / 4 = 150 packets
    e) 80 + 160 + 150 = 390
    400 - 390 = 10 packets left

# TEST 6

## Section A

1.  20 hundreds 14 tens =

    a) 2014          b) 2140
    c) 2104          d) 2410

2.  6 × _____ = 426

    a) 71            b) 24
    c) 56            d) 61

3.  1843 is 697 more than _____

    a) 3550          b) 1735
    c) 1146          d) 2540

4.  26 tens more than _____ is 8 hundreds 4 ones.

    a) 544           b) 580
    c) 1530          d) 1100

5.  9 pies were baked in every ½ h. After 4½ hours, how many pies would have been baked?

    a) 63                   b) 96
    c) 81                   d) 55

6.  There are 380 small and large marbles. The small marbles are 50 more than the large ones. How many small marbles are there?

    a) 165                  b) 185
    c) 234                  d) 215

7.  A rectangle has a breath measured 14cm and a length 18cm. What is its area?

    a) 18 cm x 4            b) 14 cm x 18 cm
    c) 14 cm x 4            d) 36 cm + 28 cm

8.  5 equal rolls of cotton wool weighed 1225g. Each of them weighed _____ g.

    a) 245                  b) 225
    c) 325                  d) 185

9.    6m 9cm - 4m 35cm =

    a) 1m 26cm        b) 1m 74cm
    c) 2m 14cm        d) 2m 55cm

10.    5/8 - 1/4 =

    a) 3/4           b) 1/4
    c) 3/8           d) 1/8

# Section B

1.   Write in words.

     4090 -

     2147 -

2.   30m = _____ cm

3.   5 kg 345g is 800g heavier than _____ kg _____ g

4.   There are 300 more oranges than apples. The oranges are twice as many as the apples. How many oranges and apples are there? _____

5.   Jane saved $132.60 last month. She saved $180 this month. How much more has Jane saved?

6.   A glass panel has a length of 960cm. Its breath is half of the length. Find the perimeter of the panel. _____ m _____ cm

7. The tuition was charged $65 for 3 hours. Peter had attended 12 hours. He had paid $_____ for his tuition.

8. Mrs. Yeo is selling every chicken wing at $1.50. She has collected $600. How many chicken wings has Mrs. Yeo sold?

9. Rearrange the numbers below. Start with the smallest.

   9148, 1098, 8069, 8108, 4069

10. Which fraction is smaller than ¼?

    1/9  1/2  3/4  7/8

11. Janet bought 1 kg 800g of butter cookies at $30. What was the weight of the cookies at $5? _____ g

12. The hawker sold 100g of vegetables at 72 cents. 900g of such vegetables cost $_____.

13.    15 groups of sixs = _____ tens

14.    Carrie was in school from 8.30am to 3.45pm. How long had Carrie been in school? _____ h _____ min

15.    Sixty 20-cent coins = $_____

# Section C

1.  Jo works part time and earns $520 monthly. She takes up another job and earns $186 weekly. How much will she earn in each month? (1 month = 4 weeks)

2.  Melissa is drawing 5 angles. She always measures each angle to be twice the one she has just drawn. Find the last angle when she has drawn a 15 degree angle for her first angle.

3.  There are 10 cars and motorcycles altogether in the repair shop. If the technician has counted a total of 32 wheels, how many motorcycles are there in the shop?

4.  Susan has made 20 bracelets. Each of the bracelets has 14 beads. Susan still has 92 beads left after making the bracelets.

    a) Find Susan's total number of beads.

    b) How many more bracelets can she make?

5. Dorothy is selling mooncakes every year. There are Two flavor the white lotus and black lotus mooncakes. She will charge more for the mooncakes with egg yolks.

The graph shows the mooncakes (with and without yolks) that Dorothy has made.

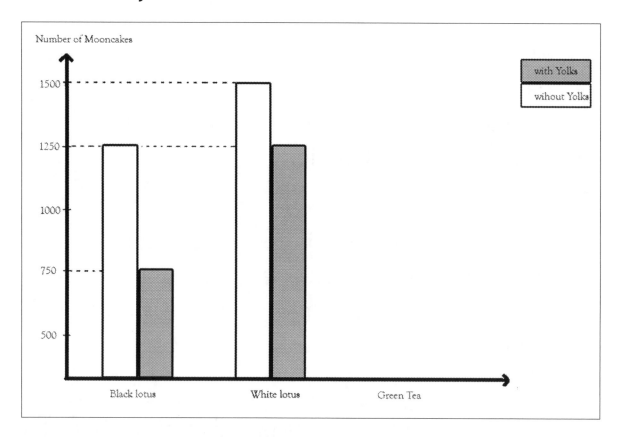

a) How many white lotus mooncakes in all has she made?

b) How many more mooncakes are there without yolks for the black lotus?

c) Dorothy is putting 4 mooncakes in a box. How many boxes of black lotus mooncakes in all has she?

d) Dorothy has a new favour of 1250 green tea mooncakes this year. Out of the green tea, there are 500 of them without yolks. Draw in the graph to show all the green tea mooncakes that Dorothy has made.

# Answers Test 6

## Section A

1. b     2. a     3. c     4. a     5. c

6. d     7. b     8. a     9. b     10. C

## Section B

1. Four thousand and ninety

Two thousand, one hundred and forty - seven

2. 3000 cm

3. 4 kg 545 g

4. 900

5. $47.40

6. 2 m 880 cm

7. $260

8. 400

9. 1098, 4069, 8069, 8108, 9148

10. 1/9

11. 300g

12. $6.48

13. 9

14. 7 h 15 min

15. $12

## Section C

1.  $186 x 4 = $744
    $744 + $520 = $1264
        She earns $1264.

2.  15 x 2 = 30

    30 x 2 = 60
    60 x 2 = 120
    120 x 2 = 240
The last angle is 240 degrees.

3.  4 motorcycles

4.  a) 20 × 10 = 200

    20 x 4 = 80
    200 + 80 + 92 = 372
    Susan's total number of beads is 372.

4.  b) 6 more bracelets

5.  a. 1500 + 1250 = 2750

    b. 1250 - 750 = 500
    c. 1250 + 750 = 2000
    2000 / 4 = 500 boxes
    d. 1250 - 500 = 750 with yolks

# TEST 7

## Section A

1. Jack bought a story book cost $8.80 and paid the cashier a $50-note. What was Jack's change?

   a) $14.12         b) $42.10
   c) $41.20         d) $32.20

2. Sandra had 496 candles in 8 boxes equally, so she had _____ candles in each box.

   a) 62             b) 54
   c) 78             d) 96

3. 9 468 = _____ hundreds _____ tens _____ ones

   a) 9... 46... 8
   b) 94... 5 ... 18
   c) 9 ... 6.. 18
   d) 90 ... 6 ... 8

4.   12m 15cm is _____ cm longer than 9m 20cm.

   a) 300                 b) 295
   c) 605                 d) 590

5.   888 divided by _____ = 4

   a) 333                 b) 222
   c) 444                 d) 111

6.   8 × 6 =

   a) 38                  b) 48
   c) 54                  d) 42

7.   5470 is _____ fewer than 9603.

   a) 3346                b) 4757
   c) 3297                d) 4133

8.   5 groups of nines is the same as

   a) 9 × 5 × 9 × 5          b) 9 x 9 x 9 x 9 x 9
   c) 5 + 5 + 5 + 5          d) 9 + 9 + 9 + 9 + 9

9.   The smallest fraction is

   a) 1/3                 b) 3/4
   c) 2/5                 d) 1/2

10. Fred has 100 pills to be taken in 25 days equally. He has to take 2 pills each time. He will be taking _____ times in a day to finish all his pills.

a) 4

b) 3

c) 2

d) 1

# Section B

1.      10 tens 3 hundreds 5 thousands is the same as _____

2.      _____, 81, 27, _____, 3

3.      Arrange in order. Begin with the greatest.

   2/3, 1/4, 1/8, 1, 1/2

4.      35 x 8 = _____ / 3

5.      The value of digit '6' in 6 284 is _____

6.      43 tens 9 ones more than 4148 is _____

7.      Draw a perpendicular line to line BE.

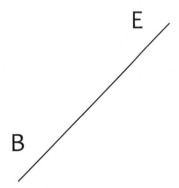

8.    9.45pm is the same as _____ mins to _____ .

9.    Susan had sold 9 purses at $3.90 each. How much did she collect for the purses? $_____

10.   8 l - 5 l 480 ml = _____ l _____ ml

11.   Each packet of sugar weighed 125g. 10 such packets of sugar weighed _____ kg _____ g.

12.   Sharon has baked 12 cupcakes. 4 of them are orange. What is the fraction of her orange cupcakes? _____

13.   490 min = _____ h _____ min

14.   The base of a square box has a length of 30cm. What is the area of the box? _____ cm sq.

15. Color 1/3 of the quarter circle.

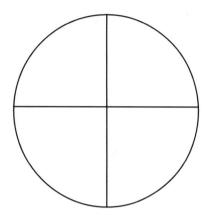

# Section C

1. 40 children are making greeting cards. 20 of them each have made 10 greeting cards. The rest of them each have made 2 cards fewer. How many cards have the children made?

2. The steamer cost $336. It was four times as expensive as the toaster. a) How much was the toaster? b) How much cheaper was the toaster?

3. Sam set the fan's timer for it to run for 120mins. After 15 mins, he stopped his fan for 1/2 hr to take his dinner.

   a. Sam finished his dinner at 6.45pm. At what time did he set the fan timer?
   b. If Sam continued to run the fan after the dinner, what time would the fan stop?

4. The wall is 2 x 3m. Johnson buys a roll of 1m wide wall paper measured 10m long. Find the wall paper that Johnson will have left after completing the whole wall.

5.  A community centre has organised various classes for its 800 members. The classes are also open to the public for non-members to participate.

Study the graph and answer the questions:

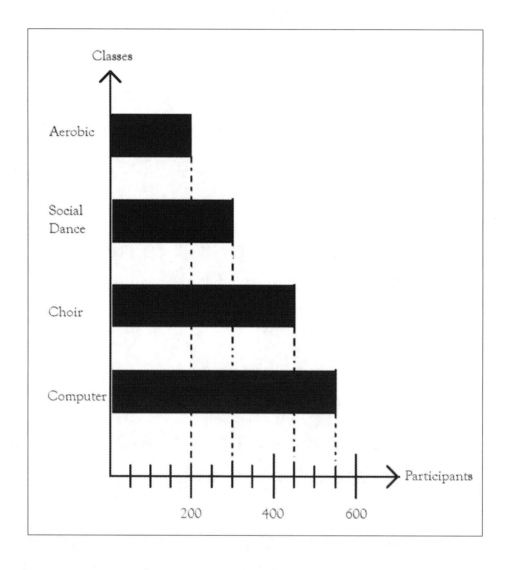

a. There are _____ participants joining the computer class and the choir.

b. There are _____ more people joining the social dance than the aerobic class.

c. The community centre has _____ participants for the four types of classes.

d. If all the community's members have joined the classes, how many participants are there in the classes NOT members ? _____

# Answers Test 7

## Section A

| | | | | |
|---|---|---|---|---|
| 1. c | 2. a | 3. b | 4. b | 5. b |
| 6. b | 7. d | 8. d | 9. a | 10. c |

## Section B

1. 5400
2. 243, 9
3. 1, 2/3, 1/2, 1/4, 1/8
4. 840
5. 6000
6. 4587
7.
8. 15 min to 10pm
9. $35.10
10. 2 l 520 ml
11. 1 kg 250 g
12. 4/12 = 1/3
13. 8 h 10 min
14. 900 cm sq
15.

## Section C

1.  20 x 10 = 200

    20 x 8 = 160

    200 + 160 = 360

    The children have made 360 cards.

2.  $336 / 4 = $84

    a. The toaster cost $84.

    $336 $84 = $252

    b. The toaster was $252 cheaper.

3.  120 mins = 2 h

    6h 45min - 30min - 15min

    a. He set the fan on at 6pm.

    6pm + 2 h + 1/2 h = 8.30pm

    b. The fan would stop at 8.30pm.

4.  10 x 1 = 10 m sq

    2 x 3 = 6 m sq

    10 6 = 4 m sq

    He has 4 m sq of the wall paper left.

5.  a. 450 + 550 = 1000

    b. 300 - 200 = 100

    c. 1000 + 300 + 200 = 1500 participants

    d. 1500 - 800 = 700 not members

Printed in the United States
By Bookmasters